All maxims and photography
by Glenn Amico

Layout and art direction by
Yahan Bermúdez

Special Thanks

Support ....The 2010 6-0 Stadium Detail

Inspiration .... Katherine Anne Pryor

Cone guidance .... Erik Sanner

Cone color consultant...Filipa Santos

Special guest appearance by .... Peter Emerick

Business support and marketing by ....Yellow 19 °

People don't change, they realize

- Michele Amico

(Michele, please don't sue Daddy)

Index

No One Reads The Preface

It was the summer of 2010, and I heard tell it was the second hottest NY summer on record. I was a sergeant assigned to the Six-O precinct in Coney Island. It was to be my last summer working for the NYPD. My 20th anniversary and retirement were looming the following April and the goal in my final 12 months was to work as much overtime as possible as well as in Coney Island summertime equated to overtime.

For my final summer, I asked to cover the circus and minor league baseball stadium. The overtime would be guaranteed every day with multiple shows daily at the circus coupled with frequent Brooklyn Cyclones home games.

When I was told that I'd be the 'stadium' sergeant, I headed for the precinct garage. My primary duty, aside from worrying about escaping elephants, would be managing traffic flow in and out of the circus and stadium. Both were located on Surf Avenue in Brooklyn, only a few blocks apart. On a good day, in the summer, Surf Avenue is a parking lot, add a couple of major events daily and you have a mess. What I was searching for in the garage were traffic cones. I studied past traffic patterns utilized for event dismissals and I had some ideas of my own but one thing I knew after 19 years as a

cop was that we needed traffic cones. In my experience, motorists tend to cooperate more with a traffic cone rather than a human standing there... Maybe it's just harder to argue with a cone. I was taken aback by the sorry state of the traffic cones at the precinct; broken, bent... half of them stolen from utility companies. So I ordered a pallet of brand-new traffic cones. When they were delivered rather than receiving praise for my initiative, the commanding officer asked somewhat emphatically "Who the fuck ordered all these freakin' traffic cones?!"
...and thus began this journey.

Introduction

traffic cone
/ˈtræfɪk kəʊn/

noun
Typically, a hollow cylindrical marker tapering
from its base. Available in various colors
depending on use or preference. For general
use they often appear in shades of orange
and can be complemented with reflective tape
thereby lending to improved visibility in dark or
darkened conditions. They are placed along
roads, footpaths or any area frequented by
vehicular or pedestrian traffic. Variously used
to temporarily redirect, separate, merge, guide,
indicate, close off, advance warn or otherwise
protect from hazards or potential dangers.

singular	traffic cone
plural	traffic cones

The Joy of Unimportance

It's a great loss to presume to know rather than care to discover.

Wanting to be gifted more than existence is a big ask.

All that I am and all that I have of value is the person I've built and what it took to get here.

Never be envious of what others have earned.

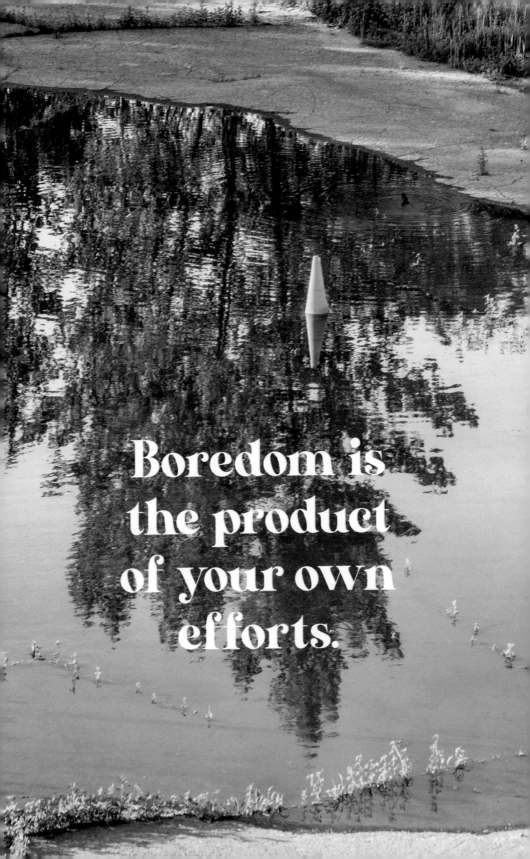

Boredom is
the product
of your own
efforts.

One must deal with the consequences of their inaction.

If confidence were
earned it wouldn't be
so easily lost.

Many are confined to "knowing what they want".

I try to be aware of
my cost to others.

Strangers do not know your narrative.

Fear of discomfort keeps those so afflicted from becoming themselves.

DANGER

THERMAL ACTIVITY

KEEP TO THE

WALKING TRACKS

AT ALL TIMES

Wilful ignorance
in the face of fear
is a commitment.

I am at peace when I'm not trying to prove or convince.

Satisfaction is attained when pleasure has limits.

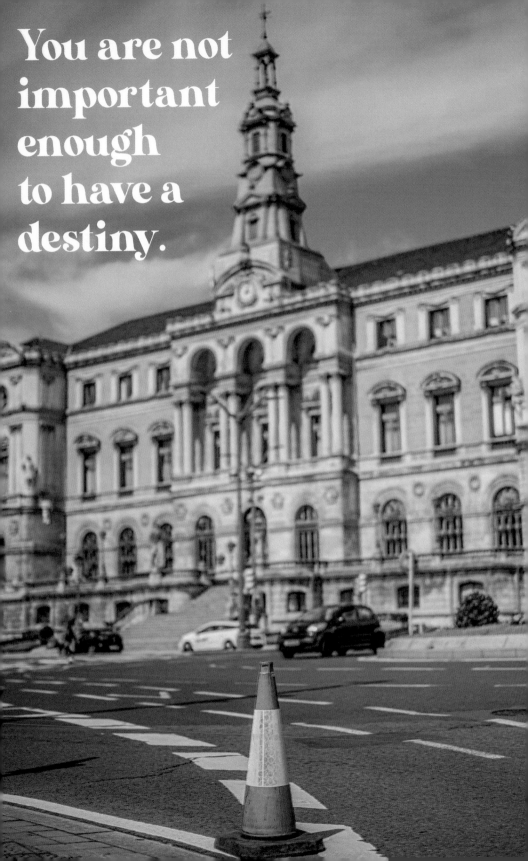

You are not
important
enough
to have a
destiny.

Your Herd Sucks

If you could tell me all there is to know about yourself, you would find it's more than you knew.

If you were to tell me all about another you'd be wrong.

Racism exists, race does not.

Protesting
is asking
others to
make the
change you
want.

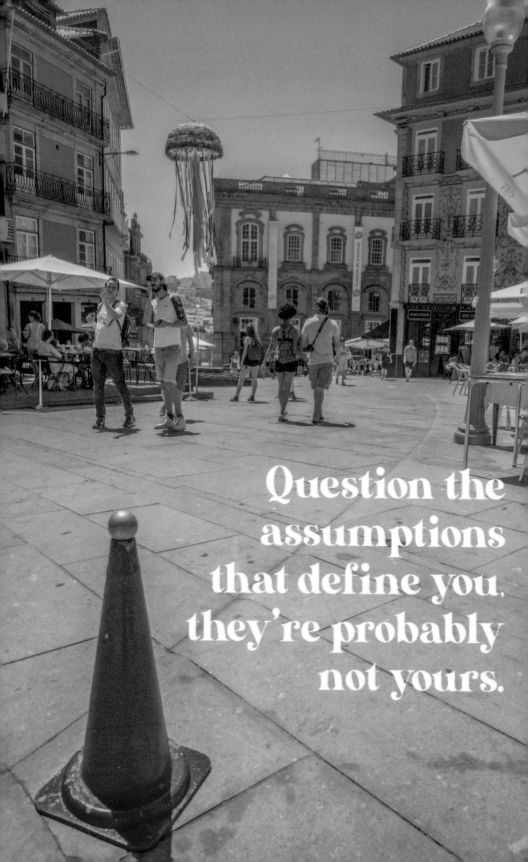

Question the
assumptions
that define you,
they're probably
not yours.

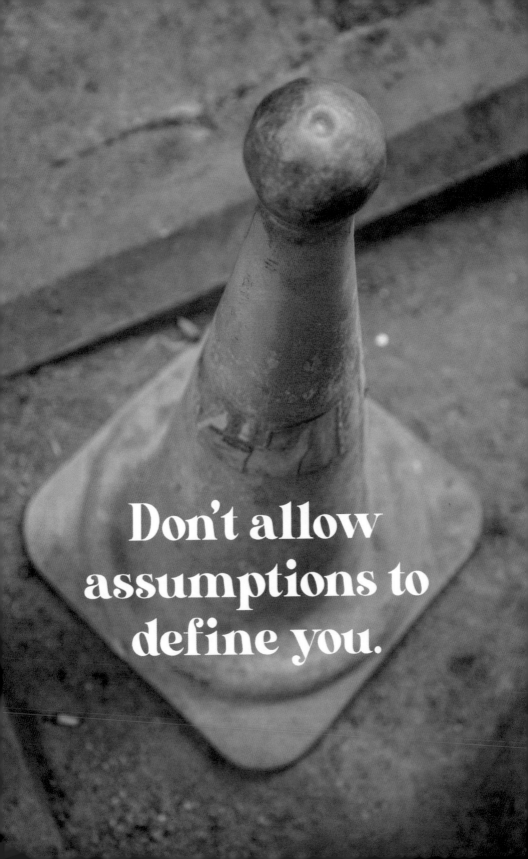

Don't allow assumptions to define you.

Moral outrage without moral action is immoral.

Nothing ends well
with an 'ism'.

After an introduction to one's list of 'ists' and 'isms', they remain a stranger.

At the very least the cost of a crowd is self-determination.

Be careful how you spend.

Popular opinion is fleeting.

Be careful where you park.

Visit cultures,
don't surrender
to them.

Unless self-
authored, all
culture is
appropriated.

Tradition and culture are the legacies of primitive peoples.

The judgemental
bear the weight
of each sentence
handed down.

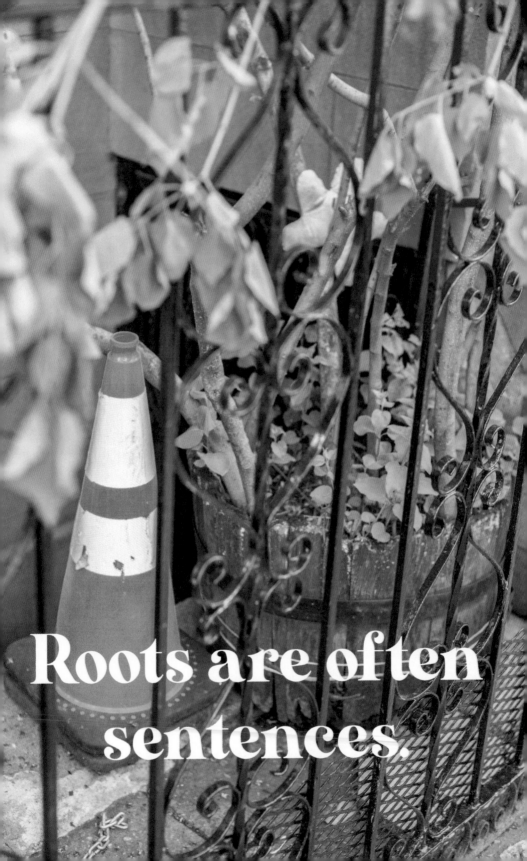

Roots are often sentences.

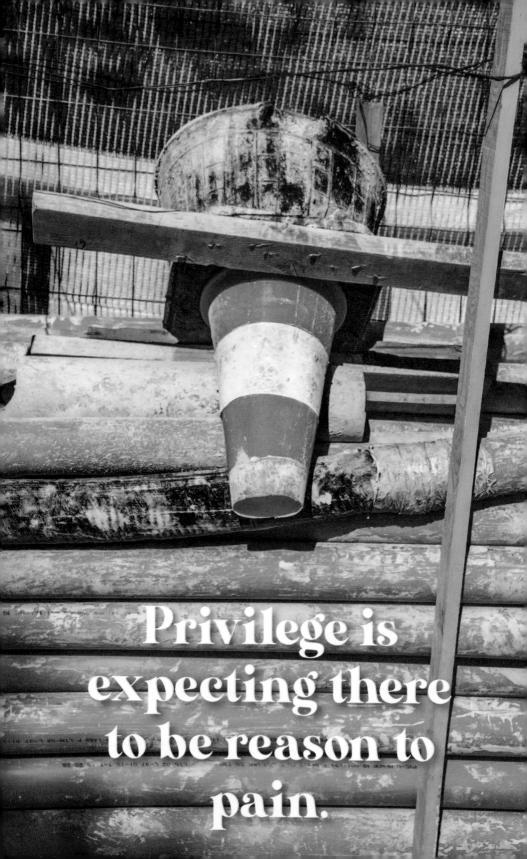

Privilege is expecting there to be reason to pain.

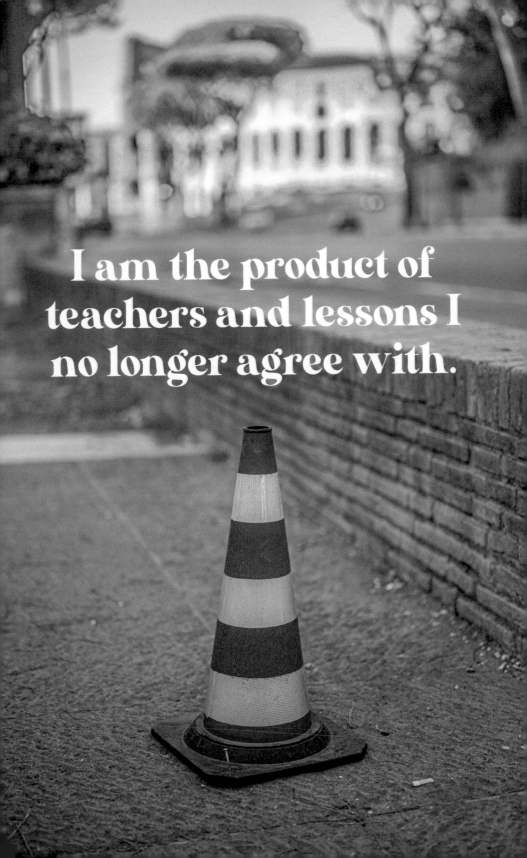

It's not honest to take pride in the accomplishments of others.

Thoughts of conspiracy are often a failure to admit to human frailty.

The problem isn't social media, it's macro us.

Aspire higher
than an echo.

The tribal are not commonly communal.

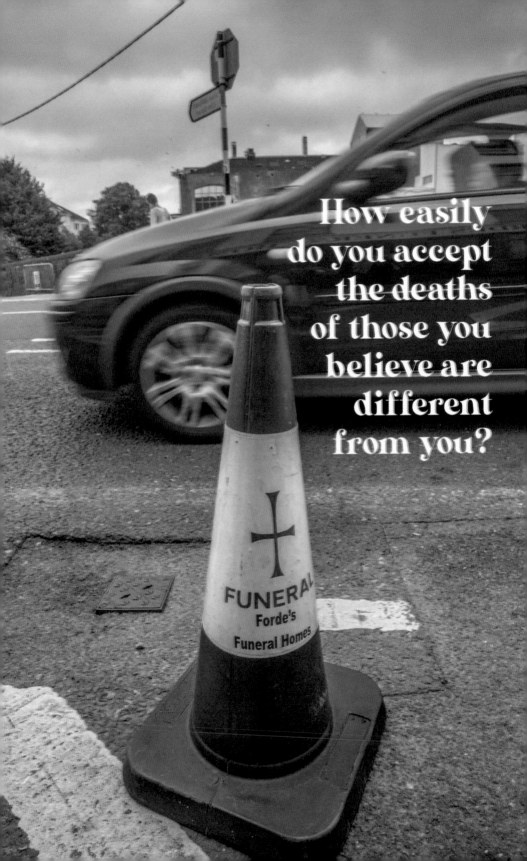

How easily do you accept the deaths of those you believe are different from you?

It's Not Magic

Maybe, if we accepted that we are only our flesh, we'd take better care.

If we realized the world is not made for us, it might not seem so unfair.

If the universe cared we'd be able to breathe in it.

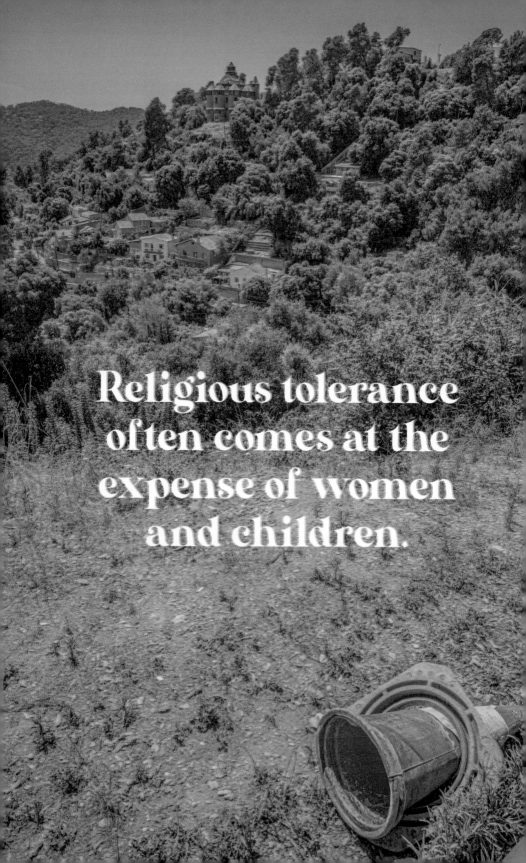

Religious tolerance often comes at the expense of women and children.

The path to an easier life?

Don't expect it to be easy.

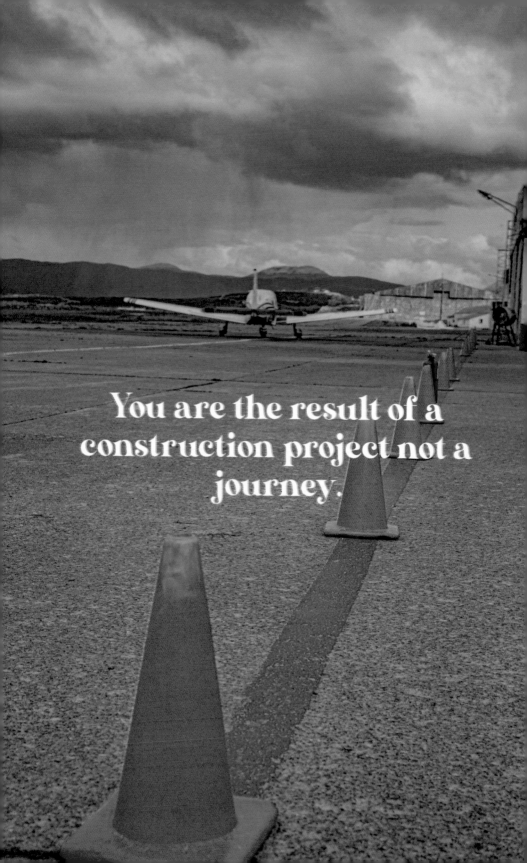

You are the result of a construction project not a journey.

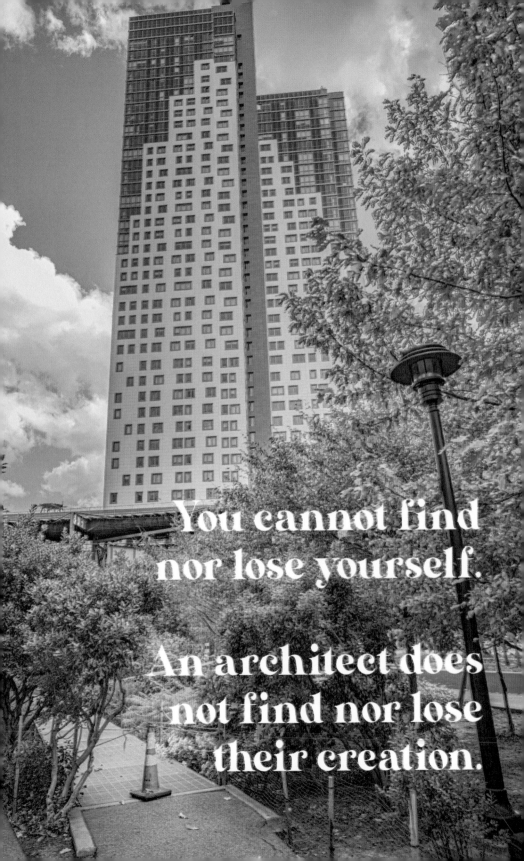

You cannot find
nor lose yourself.

An architect does
not find nor lose
their creation.

According to nature you are food... any deeper meaning needs to be self-generated.

Our perception is the smallest part of the everything that's happening.

Faith requires happenstance to be truth.

Fate dwells in
self-importance.

Freely embrace doubt,
better decisions will await.

I will always
trade a dream
for a memory.

I will always
trade magic for
understanding.

Why would the creator of the universe be concerned with your genitals?

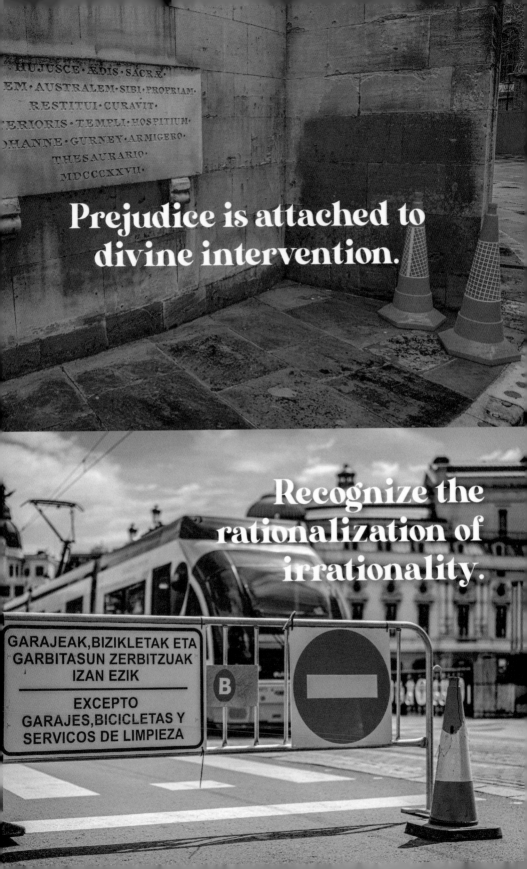

ONE WAY

Diverted K
traffic

IN

Reason not
exercised is lost.

Enlightenment is
being kind without
feeling loss.

Fulfilment is comfort with the you on display.

Often beliefs
and opinions
are presented as
actions.

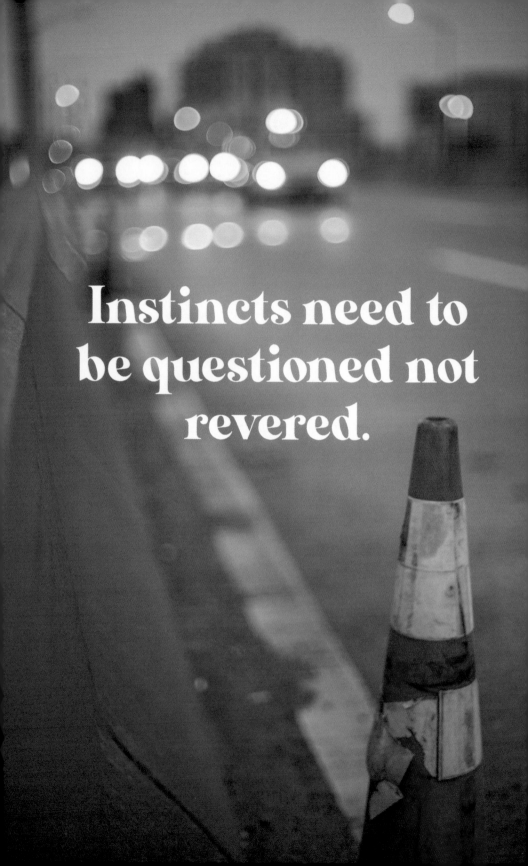

Instincts need to be questioned not revered.

If you are waiting for the happy ending, you're missing the important parts.

Security is a children's story.

You'll Die Alone and Other Thoughts on Love

The way to begin
a relationship is
alone.

Unconditional love is of little consequence. It's offered without consideration.

Soulmates are no more tangible than souls.

You can't look for
someone you don't
know. You can only
discover them.

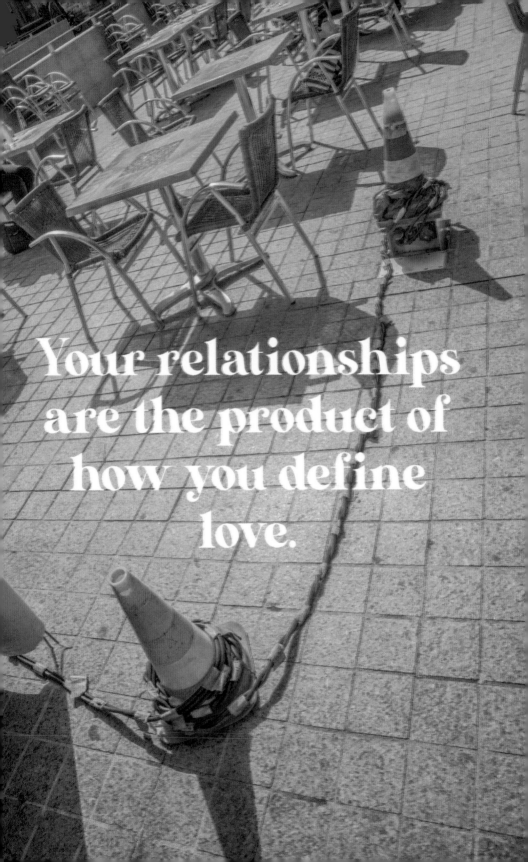

Your relationships are the product of how you define love.

Be kind despite need.

Have sex with kind people.

Rational is an aphrodisiac.

Your expectations are your own obligations.

A sustainable love is not built on a foundation of rescue.

Quite often stagnation is mistaken for growing apart.

The mention of love is meaningless without context.

An honest love can be explained.

Glenn's Handy Dandy Relationship Checklist

- ☐ **Some level of attraction**
  (At the very least it gets you talking)

- ☐ **Compatible definitions of love**

- ☐ **Similar levels of empathy**
  (Non-negotiable)

- ☐ **Complimentary value systems**
  (e.g., Bonnie and Clyde)

- ☐ **Circumstances not terribly at odds**
  (e.g., You're a vegan and they're a cannibal)

- ☐ **Some other stuff**
  (Items here are not worth mentioning if you've made it this far down the list)

NO
STANDE
OPEN RESTAUR

DINING ONLY

THE ORIGINAL
Benito One

Existential Potluck

The more you need to hide.

The more you need to hide.

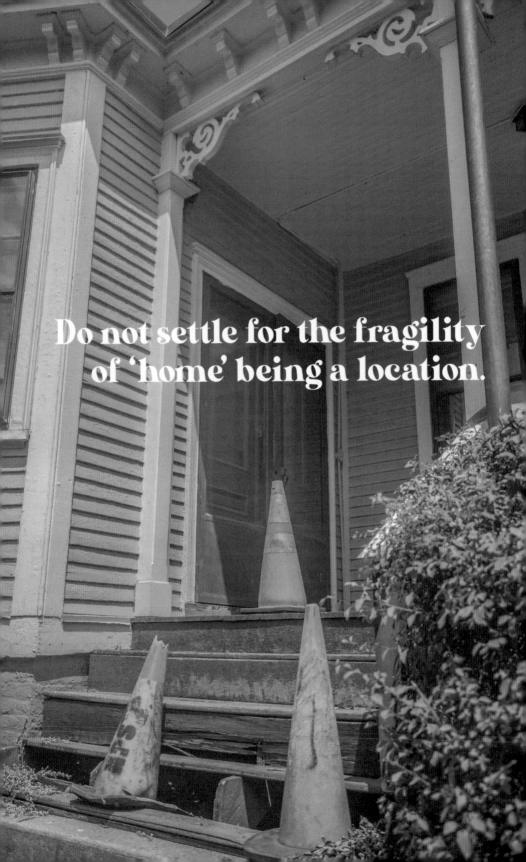

Do not settle for the fragility
of 'home' being a location.

One can sit still
in different
places.

Comfort is
best used as
a base not a
destination.

Bravery is found exclusively in the fearful.

Much is revealed in one's
assumption of malice.

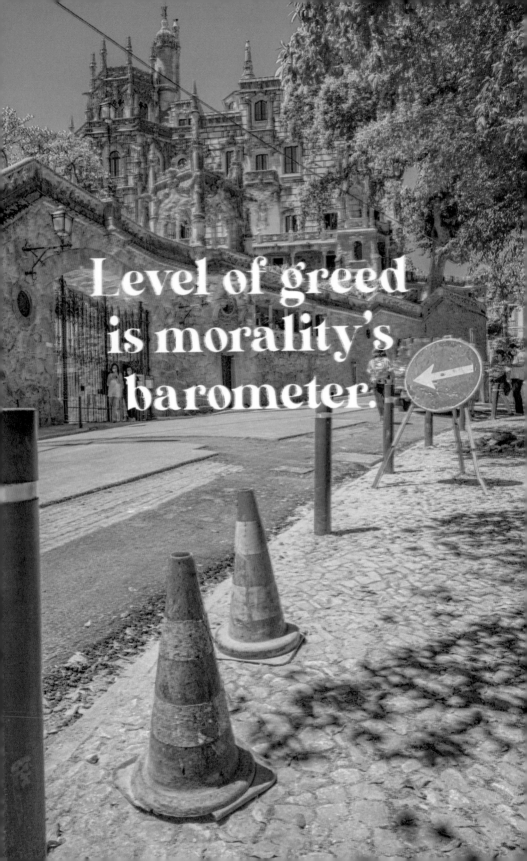

Level of greed is morality's barometer.

The duplicate of any
moment is counterfeit

Without intervention bad parenting is forever.

At any time

Facts can change but
reason is forever.

Conviction is the
map of where
you have been.

Críoch

END

"... the soup is getting cold"

About the Author

All images captured by Glenn Amico in a bunch of towns and cities, fifteen countries and seven continents.

That just about says it all.

Printed in Great Britain
by Amazon

23817262R00071